A Note to Parents and

Dorling Kindersley Readers is a compelling reading programme for beginning readers, designed in conjunction with leading literacy experts, including Cliff Moon, M.Ed., Honorary Fellow of the University of Reading. Cliff Moon has spent many years as a teacher and teacher educator specialising in reading and has written more than 140 books for children and teachers. He reviews regularly for teachers' journals.

Beautiful illustrations and superb full-colour photographs combine with engaging, easy-to-read stories to offer a fresh approach to each subject in the series. Each DK READER is guaranteed to capture a child's interest while developing his or her reading skills, general knowledge and love of reading.

The five levels of DK READERS are aimed at different reading abilities, enabling you to choose the books that are exactly right for your child:

Pre-level 1 – Learning to read

Level 1 – Beginning to read

Level 2 – Beginning to read alone

Level 3 – Reading alone

Level 4 – Proficient readers

The "normal" age at which a child begins to read can be anywhere from three to eight years old, so these levels are intended only as a general guideline.

No matter which level you select, you can be sure that you are helping your child learn to read, then read to learn!

For Dorling Kindersley

Designers Mika Kean-Hammerson,
Stefan Georgiou

Slipcase Designer Mark Penfound

Editorial Coordinator Clare Millar

Editors Matt Jones, Helen Leech,
Kate Simkins

Managing Editor Sadie Smith

Design Managers Guy Harvey,
Ron Stobbart

Pre-Production Producer
Kavita Varma

Senior Producer Charlotte Oliver

Creative Manager Sarah Harland

Publisher Julie Ferris

Art Director Lisa Lanzarini

Publishing Director Simon Beecroft

For Marvel

Editors Mickey Stern and Carl Suecoff

Reading Consultant
Cliff Moon, M.Ed.

This edition published in 2017
First published in Great Britain in 2010 by
Dorling Kindersley Limited
80 Strand, London, WC2R 0RL

A Penguin Random House Company

Slipcase UID: 001-309452-Oct/2017

A CIP catalogue record for this book is available from
the British Library.

ISBN 978-1-4053-1425-1

Printed and bound by China

marvel.com
© 2017 MARVEL

www.dk.com

A WORLD OF IDEAS:
SEE ALL THERE IS TO KNOW

DK READERS

Meet the MARVEL X-MEN

Written by Clare Hibbert

Welcome to the world of
the X-Men.
In this world, there are
some humans who seem ordinary
until they become teenagers.

Then, their special powers appear.
These kids are mutants, also known
as the X-Men.

A few humans like the X-Men and
even hope that one day everyone
will have special powers.
But most humans fear the X-Men
because they are different
from humans.

Professor X is the world's top expert
on mutants.

He is a mutant himself and has
the power to read minds.

Professor X started a school where young mutants could learn to use their powers for good.

He called his students the X-Men.

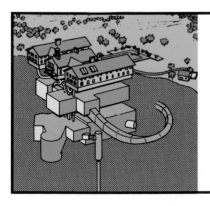

Special school
Professor X's school is no ordinary school. It has many secrets. There is even an aircraft runway.

Professor X can leave his body and travel great distances without it.

Professor X wants humans and
mutants to live together in peace.
As a young man, he was crippled in
a battle with the evil alien Lucifer.

*Professor X and
Lucifer fighting.*

Now, he moves around in
a special hoverchair that floats
just above the ground.
Professor X can send messages
into people's minds.

Scott Summers, or
Cyclops (SI-CLOPS),
was the first mutant to
join the X-Men.
His eyes send out beams
that can harm a person or
blow up a tank.
Cyclops wears special glasses to
cover his eyes.

Sentinels

The Sentinels are big
robots that were built to
destroy mutants.
They fire deadly beams
from their eyes
like Cyclops.

*Jean Grey
can move
things just
by thinking
about it.*

Jean Grey can read minds
like Professor X.
She can also make objects move
without touching them.

Jean nearly died from deadly sun
rays while flying a spaceship.
When she recovered, she became
Phoenix (FEE-NICKS).
She can use a source of energy
called the Phoenix Force.

Archangel (ARK-ANGEL) can fly like a bird.

He lost his first wings after a battle with a group of mutant fighters, the Marauders (MA-RAW-DERS).

The X-Men's enemy Apocalypse
(A-POCK-A-LIPS) gave Archangel
a new pair of metal wings.
He became one of Apocalypse's
fighters for a while.

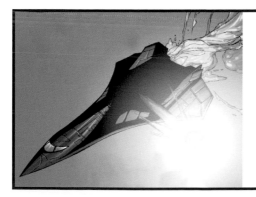

High fliers
The other X-Men
do not have wings.
They fly super-fast
jet planes called
Blackbirds.

Hank McCoy, known as the Beast,
is a clever scientist, but he looks like
a furry, blue ape.
He jumps and swings like a chimp and
has the strength of a gorilla.

When he was born, Hank seemed ordinary, except for his enormous hands and feet.

He changed into a beast when he drank a strange potion that he made in his laboratory.

Iceman can turn anything into ice,
even his own body.
He can become an ice giant and
fire weapons made of ice.
Iceman has a speedy way
to get around.
He makes a slippery ice path in
front of him and slides along.

Ice missiles
Sometimes, Iceman
makes weapons out
of ice to protect
the X-Men from
their enemies.

Nightcrawler has dark blue skin, yellow eyes and a pointy tail.
He grew up in a circus and was an amazing acrobat even before his super powers appeared.

Nightcrawler can teleport, which means he can move to another place in a second.
He can travel up to five kilometres (three miles).

Professor X found Storm in Kenya, Africa, and asked her to join the X-Men.

Storm can create rain, hail, snow and strong winds.

She can blast lightning bolts from her fingertips.

Useful gift
When she lived in Kenya, Storm used her powers to make rain to help farmers grow their crops. Because of this, the local people worshipped her as a goddess.

Professor X asked Wolverine
(WOOL-VER-EEN) to join
the X-Men.

He is a fierce fighter with
sharp claws and
superhuman hearing.

Wolverine can track a person
by smell, just like a dog.

Sharp claws
Wolverine's claws
are made of very
strong metal.
He can push them
out of his knuckles
whenever he needs
to use them.

Rogue used to belong to
the Brotherhood of Evil Mutants,
the X-Men's greatest enemies.
Then she swapped sides and
joined the X-Men.

One time, Rogue took on Wolverine's powers.

When Rogue touches someone,
they become lifeless.

She takes on all their thoughts and
powers for a short time.

She wears gloves in case
she touches someone by accident.

Magneto (MAG-KNEE-TOE) has strong magnetic powers and can lift enormous, heavy objects.

Magneto is the X-Men's biggest enemy.
He believes mutants should use their powers to take over the world.

Hideouts

Magneto has secret bases around the world and in outer space. One of his main bases is on an asteroid, a massive rock that circles the Earth.

Magneto led a band called
the Brotherhood of Evil Mutants.
One member, known as Toad,
could leap very high.

Other members were Mastermind,
who could make things that were
not real look real, and Quicksilver,
who could move very fast.

Later, the mutant Mystique
(MISS-TEEK) ran
her own Brotherhood.
The members of
her team included
Avalanche,
who could make
earthquakes, and
Destiny, who could see
into the future.

*Mystique
can change
her shape so
that she looks
like other
creatures.*

Fascinating Facts

When the X-Men member
Banshee screams,
the sound can shatter steel.

Archangel's wingspan
is 5 metres (16 feet) –
the length of
an elephant.

When he is fighting,
Nightcrawler can hold
a sword with his tail.

The strongest of
the X-Men is Colossus.
He can destroy a tank
with his bare hands.

Magneto's asteroid base
is called Avalon.
It is 250 kilometres
(150 miles) above
the Earth.

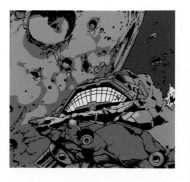